# images of NATURE

# *images of* NATURE

## THE PHOTOGRAPHS OF THOMAS D. MANGELSEN

### TEXT BY CHARLES CRAIGHEAD

HUGH LAUTER LEVIN ASSOCIATES, INC.

*I dedicate this book to my mother, Margaret Berenice, who gave me the understanding and the freedom to roam; to my father, Harold, who took me to the rivers and fields and showed me what was there; and to both of them for their unfailing support.*

Images of Nature® is a registered trademark of
Discover Wildlife Productions, Omaha, Nebraska.
For information about reproduction rights to the photographs
in this book or inquiries about limited edition prints, contact:
Images of Nature,® Post Office Box 14604, Omaha, NE 68124.

Design by Lee Riddell, Riddell Advertising & Design
Printed in Hong Kong

ISBN 0-88363-789-8

# ACKNOWLEDGMENTS

. . . . . . . . . . . . . . . . . . . . . . . . . .

I would like to thank the many people who made our book a reality.

My thanks to Charlie Craighead, whose words created beautiful images on their own. Hugh Levin, the publisher, whose support and confidence will always be appreciated and whose joyful attitude under deadline pressure will be remembered. Ron Palmer, the co-publisher, for his idea and initial interest in doing the book. Lee Riddell, for putting it all together, for her creative design and unending patience, and for caring so much. Ed Riddell, for his artistic eye and constant willingness to give needed advice.

I am also greatly indebted to my brother, David, who believed in my photography from the beginning and gave so much to make it all possible. Kathy Watkins and Dan Fulton, for their support and wonderful companionship in the field and for their organization and valuable assistance at the editing table. Margaret Murie, for her kind words and many years of inspiration. Paul Johnsgard, who took me under his wing in graduate school and first inspired me to pick up a camera. Nancy Kendrick, for convincing me that there are many choices in life. David Lenz, for his assistance and companionship on the Platte River. My grandfather, David Alexander, and my brothers, Bill and Hal, for their encouragement and valuable suggestions. Bert Kempers, for his confidence in me and for giving me my first photography job. Rod Drewien, Ernie Kuyt, and Gene Steffen, for their help in photographing the whooping cranes. My friends and guides in Africa, Yakub, Guchanja, Ali, and Peter.

Special appreciation is due to Robert Porath, Louise Lasley, Ellin Yassky Silberblatt, Dale Ramsey, Kerry Lamb, Maryellen Carlman, Lisa Bolton, Julie McIntyre, Marietta Lanphear, Magda Malachowski, Dale Upshaw, Ginna Bousum, Caroline Muller, Katherine Buell, Jerry Walker, Roy and Owen Gromme, Helen and Bob Grennan, Michael Fitzpatrick, Ellery and Donna Lenz, Wayne and Dorothy Schneider, Jon Stuart, Bob and Inger Koedt, Herman Weist, Richard O'Connor, Ellen Martin, Clarence and Dodie Stearns, and Bert and Meg Raynes.

My thanks also to the staff of Images of Nature galleries for giving me their support and the time that I dedicated to this book. In particular, I would like to thank Mary Rommelfanger, Shirley Nebel, Karen Digilio, Debbie Day, and Nancy Fredericks.

I also thank the U.S. Fish and Wildlife Service and the National Park Service for their help and cooperation.

To the many others who have helped in various ways and whom I have inadvertently forgotten and will remember after it is too late—thank you.

—*Thomas D. Mangelsen*

. . . . . . . . . . . . . . . . . . . . . . . . . .

# FOREWORD
## *images of the artist*

· · · · · · · · · · · · · · · · · · · · · · · · · · · · · · · · ·

onsider a biologist turned photographer. Here is a heady combination—
a double power. A biologist must have strong powers of observation,

endless patience, a great interest in and sense of harmony with all living

things, from elephants to the tiniest flower. All this the photographer must

also have, along with knowledge of cameras, of lenses, and of lights and

shadows. 🦢 Tom Mangelsen has all these traits, and among them I would

rank his endless patience as the most important. 🦢 Some of Tom's pictures

are almost unbelievable. In them it seems as if the subjects were cooperating

in a conscious way. This has to be called "luck," I suppose, but I think the

photographer must have a magical sensitivity that leads him to the right spot

at the right moment. How else could it happen? 🦢 The shot of the Alaskan

brown bear and the salmon on the cover of this book looks impossible, of

course, so I am sure it must have sprung from that same magic—the combination

of sharp observation and endless patience, with camera always on the ready.

🦢 I can't imagine the feeling of satisfaction that must warm the heart

· · · · · · · · · · · · · · · · · · · · · · · · · · · · · · · · ·

*Trumpeter swans find warmth for their heads by tucking them under their wings in sub-zero temperatures. Mist rising from water nearby condenses and freezes on their plumage.*

*Trumpeter swans mate for life and return each spring to the same nesting territory where they reinforce their pair bond through courtship displays.*

*FRONTISPIECE
With his new antler growth covered in velvet, a bull elk drinks from a tributary of the Yellowstone River, where geothermally warmed water creates mist on cool summer mornings.*

*A fearless hunter of small rodents, the ermine—a short-tailed weasel in its white, winter phase—sometimes attacks prey as large as a snowshoe hare. The pure white fur will be shed for a brown coat in the spring.*

of the photographer when he knows that he has captured not only the physique of an animal, but the animal in place in its habitat. I found myself gazing for a long time at the little winter ermine and feeling entranced by its at-home and serene "personality" in its proper setting.

To make this book a complete work of art, we have Charles Craighead's sensitive interpretations and comments. I have known Charlie all his life, and it is a real satisfaction to read his sympathetic words.

Tom and Charlie have given us an abiding delight. This book will take you all over the world. Turn the pages with joy.

And be thankful for patient people!

—*Margaret E. Murie*

Margaret E. Murie is one of North America's most respected voices in the effort to preserve wilderness. She spent nearly forty years living in the remote regions of the Rocky Mountains and Alaska studying wildlife with her husband, the renowned biologist and wilderness spokesman Olaus Murie. Her concern for the natural world has inspired three generations of naturalists.

# CONTENTS

# INTRODUCTION
## *images of an interior landscape*

. . . . . . . . . . . . . . . . . . . . . . . . . . . . . . . . . . . . . . . . . . .

I n the first, faint light of a fifteen-degree winter morning, photographer Tom Mangelsen straps on his snowshoes and starts through deep snow toward a tree-lined riverbank, where mist rises slowly into the air. He carries a heavy tripod with a camera and a telephoto lens and a backpack filled with film, lenses, and spare batteries. Another camera hangs around his neck. His coat pockets bulge with extra gloves, smaller wide-angle lenses, binoculars, and a daily journal. His breath condenses and freezes on his collar. From a bridge a mile upstream Mangelsen has observed river otters catching fish the past two mornings. Photographs of otters are needed for a pending magazine article, but he also hopes to get an image good enough for a limited-edition print. He is headed for the bend in the river where he last saw the otters and hopes to be set up before they arrive to fish. Just before the sun rises, he reaches the river and peers carefully over the snowy riverbank at the water. No otters are in sight. Finding a spot where he can set up the tripod where only the long lens will be

. . . . . . . . . . . . . . . . . . . . . . . . . . . . . . . . . . . . . . . . . . .

*Dense thickets of willow grow in the moist bottom-land soil of a mountain valley. The fast-growing shrubs are browsed back each year by wintering moose, and they are a favored food of the beavers that flood the thickets with their dams.*

*Banking sharply to dive after a salmon, a mature bald eagle displays the white head that inspired its name. The distinctive white feathers appear when the eagles are four or five years old.*

CONTENTS

*One of the most graceful of flyers, a herring gull hovers effortlessly in the wind while exploring the shoreline for food.*

*Winging from one feeding spot to another, trumpeter swans give their loud, horn-like call. The swans may winter near their northern nesting grounds if there is sufficient open water.*

visible from the water, he waits in the morning stillness. Soon a raven calls from its roost in a spruce tree, and then a small flock of goldeneyes whistles past. The river community has come to life.

Mangelsen spends the morning waiting patiently for the otters to show up. Across the river, only a hundred feet away, he can see their tracks and the remains of fish from yesterday. He knows otters can cover miles of river in their daily travels and could appear at any time, and he thinks of what he missed the last two mornings when he was unable to snowshoe out to the river. While he waits, he takes a few pictures of a bald eagle circling in the distance. The morning sky is dramatic, but he won't know if he has caught the bird in a majestic pose until the film is processed; gloved hands and an eyepiece fogged by cold make the exact timing of the shutter release difficult.

By ten o'clock the otters still have not shown up, and the beautiful morning light has given way to harsh winter sky. Mangelsen packs up and mentally schedules himself to try again the next morning. Having the rest of the day to photograph, he thinks about other nearby possibilities for wildlife that would be productive in late afternoon or evening light. He starts slowly downstream, watching and listening from the riverbank. He decides to work his way to an oxbow bend in the river, where he suspects the otters may have their den in an old muskrat burrow. There, too, waterfowl congregate on the calm, open water, and other wildlife find shelter in the surrounding willows and forest. Even in the bright light of midday there may be chances for good images along the water's edge and in the open shadows of the trees.

After snowshoeing slowly for a half-mile along the river, Mangelsen hears the deep, hornlike call of trumpeter swans coming from downstream. The anxious sound indicates that they are in flight, so he kneels and readies his camera, focusing on the far bend in the river and quickly selecting a shutter speed and aperture. Then four of the huge, white swans fly gracefully around the bend and head toward him. He begins firing his motor-driven camera in short sequences, critically focusing and adjusting the composition as the swans approach. Knowing they will rise and turn when they see him, he steadies himself and waits until their formation and the position of their broad wings are right before shooting the last few frames. As they bank away from him into blue sky, he finishes the roll with a series of images of the swans in closeup.

To the southwest there is a wall of blowing snow as a small local storm moves out of the mountains and across the valley. Mangelsen estimates he will meet the storm at the oxbow bend and, still hoping to find the otters, visualizes a photograph of dark otters in a brief, driving snow. He short-cuts through a stand of old cottonwoods and young spruce trees, stopping to eat lunch on a fallen cottonwood and waiting for the light to improve as the snowstorm approaches. While he eats, he watches mountain chickadees flitting in the trees and hears a downy woodpecker rattling in the dead bark

*A downy woodpecker's stiff tail holds it erect as it drills for insect larvae, eggs, and cocoons.*

of one of the cottonwoods. He knows he already has better images of these birds than he could get in today's light, so he just sits still and watches, enjoying the company of the birds.

Out of the corner of his eye he sees a flash of white and turns to see an ermine, the white, winter phase of a weasel, standing boldly on the other end of the log. The little weasel is unafraid and curious, but it rarely stops long enough in its hunt for food to have its picture taken. Mangelsen slowly reaches for the camera resting on his pack and is surprised when the ermine stays put. He quickly takes a few shots and, when the ermine still doesn't flee, he leans forward to compose a new background. The ermine bounds off the log, and Mangelsen follows to the base of a dense spruce tree where the ermine dives into a dark hollow. When it reappears a second later, Mangelsen is focused and waiting, and he finishes the roll of film before the animal turns and runs. Excited about the unexpected good luck, Mangelsen leaves for the oxbow with the exposed film tucked safely in his shirt pocket.

When he arrives at the water's edge, the afternoon light is beginning to improve. Light snow is falling, and sunlight is burning through a corner of the storm, giving color and depth to the surroundings. The only thing missing is the otters. Mangelsen sets up and waits. The sky and scenery continue to look better, so he starts taking pictures of the landscape with its storm, river reflections, and falling snow.

Finally, as the western sky turns pink and the temperature starts to drop, he sees the familiar shapes of the otters working their way upriver, swimming porpoise-like, diving below and arcing above the surface. He watches in frustration as the otters seem to dawdle deliberately, as the light fades, and he constantly checks his light meter and makes adjustments in preparation. Just as the light drops below the limit for a shutter speed fast enough to freeze the otters in their mercurial activities, they slide up onto the ice barely fifty feet away. The last otter out of the water carries a whitefish, and the animals devour it, then roll in the snow and wrestle playfully. Mangelsen can only watch with mixed feelings of fascination and frustration; the photographer in him tries to think of a way to get something other than a dark, blurry picture, while the naturalist in him enjoys the intimate encounter. The otters move off the ice and swim upriver, and Mangelsen packs his cameras.

Snowshoeing back to his car, he reviews his day's images and reminds himself to feel positive about the results despite the disappointing conclusion. He regrets missing the otters by only a few minutes, but the pictures of the ermine and the landscape and storm at the oxbow will definitely be good, and the swans and the bald eagle are possible prints. He has been doing this long enough to know that he should not worry about missed opportunities, especially with a wild and free-roaming subject like wildlife. It also presents a challenge to return tomorrow to try for the images he saw while the otters played in fading light.

Most professional wildlife photographers would have difficulty pinpointing exactly when or how it became a career. Once it did, few would

*The berries of the mountain ash remain on the tree through the winter and are an important food source for late-nesting birds like the cedar waxwing.*

and other birds, Mangelsen adhered to his biological training and made sure that the scene was correct, that the animal was doing what came naturally and that it was portrayed in its normal habitat. This led to his frequent use of the local climate to underscore the conditions in the animal's environment. He began to turn fog, clouds, rain, and snow into essential elements of the photograph. "I realized I couldn't wait for the sun to shine for dramatic lighting and that animal activity went on whether it was raining, snowing, or blowing. I began to find that the animals were remarkable reflections of the mood of the weather by their positions and appearance. They also tended to be less concerned about me if their activities were strongly influenced by the weather. There was a big difference between a bird sitting on a limb in bright summer sunshine and the same bird hunkered down on a frozen branch with its feathers puffed up in twenty-below-zero weather."

From that development, Mangelsen proceeded to incorporate more and more of the environmental conditions into his scenes until, in some instances, the bird or mammal became a minor part of the image. Such landscapes of wildlife habitat may contain only a small silhouette or a distant but recognizable animal shape, but nevertheless convey all the intense feeling of a close-up action photograph.

Still, Mangelsen may be best known for his natural depiction of animal behavior. He finds animals feeding, calling a mate, or caught in a posture that suggests impending flight. He relies on his training as a biologist to recognize and record bits of behavior that accentuate the images' naturalism. His picture of a sea otter floating on its back sleeping shows the otter's habit of wrapping itself in kelp to keep the tides from drawing it out to sea, and his photographs of flocks of bright waxwings clustered on a mountain ash tree were recorded when the birds made their annual search for late-ripening berries in sub-zero temperatures.

Anticipating behavior and where it will lead an animal in relation to a background is what gives Mangelsen the compositions he wants. Years of watching and learning the movements of animals has developed his ability to bring together the photographic process and natural behavior at the chosen scene. Many of his images are made when an animal moves into the camera's view, as if on a set, rather than when the animal is followed until it holds still. Mangelsen's images thus give the impression of being the view of an invisible bystander in a natural drama. This attribute comes from taking time not only to learn the habits of the subject, but also to allow it to become accustomed to an outside presence.

It all derives from patience, a quality Mangelsen learned by hunting with his father along the Platte River. "If you could hunt ducks and geese with Harold," he remarks, "you could wait for anything. Watching all day for an eagle to catch a salmon is nothing compared to sitting in Dad's goose blind. Patience usually has its reward, but in photography you have to know what that reward is going to be. You have to do more than just sit somewhere and wait for something to happen. When I was in Denali photographing grizzlies as they hunted arctic ground squirrels, I saw the possibility for an image that would be worth waiting for. Even though the chance was remote and it would take a lot of luck, I knew it was a matter of spending the time to get the picture I wanted of a huge and powerful grizzly closing in on a small ground squirrel. The action may be brief and hard to see, but I hoped that eventually a squirrel might flee in the open, and in the right direction and distance from the bear, to make it a chase. I was lucky, but I had to wait and work for it."

The most beneficial use of his wildlife biology work is his understanding of the relationships of animals and plants and of how to find one subject in conjunction with another. Because his subject matter is free and wild, there are no guarantees that a trip for a specific animal will be productive. So Tom must know which other species can be found in a given vicinity and be prepared if his primary subject is not accessible or if the arrival or departure of a migratory species has not been as expected. One of his more popular prints is that of a robin—not really considered a great subject by most wildlife photographers—that appeared while Mangelsen was waiting for a flock of Bohemian waxwings to move to a berry-laden tree near his camera. The result was an image revealing the robin as a wild thrush instead of as a familiar lawn decoration. Another time, while waiting for fog to lift from a marsh so that he could look for cranes, Mangelsen watched black-necked stilts wading in the dense mist. He could barely see them through the viewfinder but started photographing anyway, hoping something recognizable would come through the thick fog. His result was a beautiful, eerie image of two black-necked stilts stepping delicately in the mist.

Working in national parks and wildlife sanctuaries has imbued in Mangelsen a strong belief in the need for the conservation of natural resources. He actively supports the efforts of many groups and donates his photographic skills when possible. "It's not just a matter of trying to protect the basis for my occupation by helping wildlife," he says. "My photography is a way of showing people what's out there. If I can get people to feel what I do when I see a great gray owl or a loon, then it's that much easier to convince them we need to protect these things. If my photography career had not developed I'd be out there with the same goal, but possibly painting, sculpting, or doing research."

Mangelsen keeps in contact with many wildlife research projects and works jointly with biologists to promote studies of rare or endangered species. In 1984 he filmed and helped produce a National Geographic television special, *Flight of the Whooping Crane,* which depicted the migration of the rare birds and the efforts to save them from extinction. He found the film especially rewarding to make. "The whooping crane was historically found along the Platte during migrations from their wintering grounds to nesting areas in the north. I grew up with sandhill cranes on the Platte but never saw whoopers. It was a great satisfaction to be able to contribute to the effort to make people aware of the beautiful cranes and of the scientists' efforts to bring them back

*Wading gracefully through their marshy home, black-necked stilts feed in the shallow water. Among shore-birds, stilts have the longest legs in proportion to body size.*

*Whooping cranes hovered on the edge of extinction for years, but recent protection and management have brought a gradual comeback for one of the rarest and most celebrated birds. In 1941, only fifteen of these cranes were known to exist.*

*Sandhill cranes mass for their evening roost in the shallow Platte River, where the current discourages predators. The Platte and surrounding land is critical for migrating cranes to gain strength and reaffirm pairs.*

from near-extinction. I feel the real purpose of my work is to convince people to save what natural beauty and wildlife we still have."

In wind-driven snow, Tom Mangelsen's camera sits on its tripod protected by a waterproof cover, but the photographer huddles behind a snowdrift to escape the brunt of the storm. Still, the cold powder sifts down his neck and over his face. Watching a flock of waterfowl from the bridge, he had seen otters far downstream during a lull in the blizzard. So he had quickly loaded his pack and snowshoed out to the river. Now, as the storm closes in again and he has to sit unmoving, he begins to feel the chill. He thinks of a warmer coat left behind in the car and the thermos bottle of hot coffee forgotten on the seat. Then the chirping call of the otters reaches him, and as the sound seems to come closer on the wind, he peers over the snowdrift. There is nothing but blowing snow and the dark water of the river. The otters are out there, but only luck will bring a break in the storm when the animals arrive. Tom Mangelsen pulls his collar closer and wraps his arms over his knees—and he waits.

# WATERSIDE
## *images of coast and shoreline*

. . . . . . . . . . . . . . . . . . . . . . . . . . . . . . .

*Sunset on the Pacific coast colors the sky over Monterey Bay, California.*

*The serrated edges of its bill keep a common puffin's catch of fish secure as it returns to its burrow nest. Puffins use their stubby wings as fins to "fly" under-water in pursuit of fish, and when they catch a fish it is pinched and then held until the bill is full.*

Coastal life mirrors the cyclic tides and seasonal nature of the ocean. Animals appear and disappear in phenomenal numbers, migrating to breeding grounds or congregating for seasonal sources of food. There is a full range of life forms, from birds to fish to carnivorous mammals. There are colossal whales and microscopic plants, predators and prey. The sea tempers the air and nourishes plants, its influence pushing inland until mountains halt the flow of moisture. This is a rich zone of briny water and lush plant growth, of bounty and famine both. A brief squall moves from the open sea into a cold Alaskan bay. Dense sheets of rain march toward the shoreline, pushed by gusts of wind. The rain spatters unnoticed in the surf, pounds the sand, and washes salt spray from the beach vegetation. It carries far inland where it blurs the air and drips from great trees. After the storm, fog and a light rain fill the summer sky. From the swells of the sea a gray whale breaches and sounds. Its tail hangs in the air briefly, dripping sea water, then slips gracefully into the depths. A school of sockeye

. . . . . . . . . . . . . . . . . . . . . . . . . . . . . . .

*Its seven-foot wingspan carries a bald eagle on a flight along the Alaskan coast in search of fish.*

salmon mills in the deep water offshore, waiting for the tides to push them up into the stream of their origin. As fingerlings they entered salt water four years ago to begin their transformation into sleek sea creatures. They explored the fathoms of the oceans, and some carry scars from seals and sea otters or from predatory fish. The weak have been sifted from the school. Now the salmon return to breed and die in their native fresh water. They no longer eat, intent only on surviving the shock of fresh water and the upstream battle to calm pools. Their powerful bodies are changing once again, now growing humped and hooked and turning crimson. With a tidal surge, the school swarms up into the glacial stream.

On the dead snag of a huge coastal spruce, a bald eagle sits hunched in the downpour. Instinctively it scans the dense coastal vegetation and meandering stream, watching for prey. A dark shadow moving in the stream below causes the eagle to sit erect and focus sharply; the school of sockeyes moves in deep water along one shore where the overhanging vegetation protects them. They burst from cover into a wide, shallow riffle, headed for the deeper water. Their dorsal fins break the surface as they splash through the shallows, and the eagle leans into the wind. Becoming airborne, it tucks into a long, shallow dive that levels out just above the water. Its powerful feet and sharp talons reach forward to pull a thrashing salmon out of the water, and the eagle carries it heavily across the river to a gravel bar.

The eagle's arrival frightens a flock of western sandpipers, which lift noisily into the air and zigzag downstream to the beach. They settle at the water's edge and begin following the ebb and flow of the surf, searching for food in the exposed shallows. The eagle feeds on its salmon, then flaps upward, slowly circling over the stream. It joins another eagle drifting high over snowfields and glaciers above the steep coastal valley. Soon there will be thousands of eagles drawn to the spawning salmon.

The leading salmon press on, unaware of the feast in their wake. Their numbers diminish as they encounter river otter and mink and then the brown bears that wait in the last cascades before the spawning beds. The migrating salmon will finally reach the headwaters where, once their eggs are laid in the gravel, their life cycle will end. Then the decomposing bodies of the sockeyes will nourish new life as they begin to drift downstream to the sea.

*The streamlined flukes of a gray whale drip sea water, and its tail hangs briefly in the air as it dives after surfacing to breathe.*

The hermit thrush nests on the ground in the moss and grass of coastal forests and thickets. It is considered to have one of the most beautiful songs of any North American bird.

*Bizarre facial patterns mark the harlequin, a small duck that nests along turbulent mountain streams and winters in stormy coastal water.*

FOLLOWING PAGES
Sunrise finds a young white-tailed deer poised where it has come to feed on plants at the water's edge.

A shy bird of ponds and waterways, the green-backed heron can often be seen poised motionlessly watching for prey or moving cat-like through shallow water, one stealthy step at a time, grabbing small fish in its bill.

A black oystercatcher in Prince William Sound waits for a receding tide to uncover mussels and clams, which it pries open with the tip of its chisel-like bill. Catastrophic oil spills are especially devastating to the fragile intertidal zone and the birds that feed there.

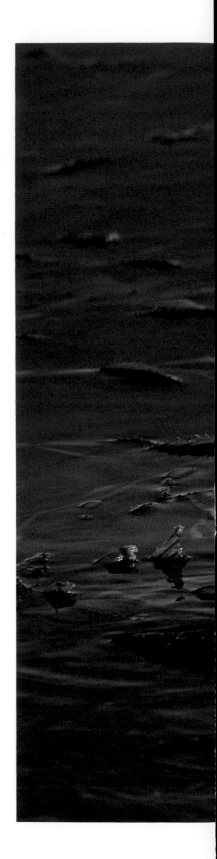

*Offshore rocks offer a
harbor seal safe sunbathing
in Monterey Bay.*

*After feeding on sea urchins
and crabs, a napping sea
otter wraps itself in the kelp
of Monterey Bay to keep
from drifting away. Tiny
bubbles trapped in the
otter's dense fur keep it
warm and afloat.*

*PREVIOUS PAGES
A Louisiana, or tri-colored,
heron watches for fish in
tidal channels and marshes
of the southern United
States. The heron often
hunts by running in
shallow water or stirring
the bottom with one foot to
flush its prey.*

*A ring-billed gull stretches*
*while waiting for afternoon*
*winds and tides to arrive so*
*it can hunt for food.*

*Each spring, common puffins return to land from the open sea, then choose mates and dig their burrow nests on rocky headlands. When the young are fully grown, they are abandoned in the burrow, and the parents fly back out to sea.*

*Black-legged kittiwakes are small, graceful gulls that build deeply cupped nests on sheer sea cliffs. They nest in large colonies along the northern coasts and on offshore islands.*

*The moods associated with the meeting of the churning sea and the land would not be complete without the gulls that ride the winds of approaching storms.*

*FOLLOWING PAGES*
*Daisies growing along a lakeshore add their subtle color to the brief summer of northern Maine.*

*Loons, which nest on the islands and shorelines of pristine lakes, are considered a sign of undisturbed wilderness. Because they live on the fish of northern lakes, loons are susceptible to the contaminants in acid rain.*

*Distinct markings and a ruby eye distinguish the common loon. Loons have solid bones and dense bodies that enable them to sink below the surface without a ripple in pursuit of fish.*

# COMMON LOON
## *notes from the field*

For some reason, like many people I have a special attraction to loons. Maybe it is their color and shape, their haunting call, or the wild regions of woods and water where they live. The Maine North Woods is one such region. There one finds an area that seems to be almost half water and half woods—a real maze of lakes, streams, marshes and forests cover the landscape. I wanted to see this country and photograph the loons, so my companion and fellow photographer Kathy Watkins and I did some research on the area and on the habits of the loons. Learning where to go, getting there, and setting up are often the biggest challenges of nature photography.

We went to one of the region's largest lakes. A gravel road took us to the shore, and there in the woods, chained to a tree, was the small fishing boat we had arranged to have as our transportation for the next five days. Our quarters, an old fishing shack, we were told, was "about a half-mile east of the stashed boat by way of an old logging road now grown over and hard to find, or a bit farther by boat, around some shallow, rocky shoals between a couple of small islands, around a point of land, and you're there."

Those directions and our pile of heavy gear made the longer route by boat sound like the easy way, and since we needed the boat to explore the lake anyway, we loaded it up. We piled in our camera gear, sleeping bags, tent, life vests, food, and our last four beers. I poured the mixture of gas and oil into the three-horsepower motor, jerked on the cord a dozen times, pushed the lever to reverse, and in a cloud of wonderful-smelling blue smoke we were off— just long enough to get our bow off the shore and hear the motor sputter to a stop. In the abrupt silence a scolding red squirrel seemed to taunt us from his tree. I untangled the mass of water lily roots cinched around the propeller, pulled on my rubber waders, and got out to pull the boat to deeper water. Feeling a rush of cold water on my left leg, I remembered the hole in my boot behind the knee. As far back as I can remember, it has seemed natural to have cold, wet feet, even with wading boots. My dad would say, "Just wiggle your toes."

Beyond the tangle of vegetation, we were on our way

*The haunting, laughter-like call of the common loon is an unforgettable sound of the northern wilderness. Their wailing cries at night, echoing across moonlit lakes, gave rise to the expression "crazy as a loon."*

*Seemingly able to walk on water, a young white-tailed deer bounds across the shoals of a shallow lake.*

## notes from the field *(continued)*

at last, watching a beautiful sunset and what looked like the silhouette of a loon in the distance on the mirrorlike water. Loon country! Suddenly I heard the scraping of our aluminum hull against the rocks and the pop of the propeller jumping out of the water. I'd been here before: cold, wet feet, water too shallow to motor the boat—it was another Mangelsen adventure.

Kathy and I took turns pulling the boat toward a "hot meal in our cabin in the woods." We passed by a half-dozen islands before we found water deep enough to run the motor. Slowly, we rounded point after point, squinting into what seemed total darkness for a sign of our cabin. By now we were wet and cold from our waists down, the price of finding deeper water. (I remembered an executive I had met in my gallery a week earlier; envious of my career, he had wanted to trade jobs. *Now* I was willing!) In such circumstances one learns a lot about a traveling companion's personality. Anyone still able to laugh, as Kathy was, is worth having along.

In desperation we fumbled in our packs and found a flashlight. It was the small backpacker kind that campers use to find a toothbrush at the bottom of their packs. Kathy pointed it directly toward shore, which made us laugh, because the beam of light barely reached the bow of the boat. About the time we were ready to turn back, we saw the cabin.

We built a fire to warm ourselves and dry our clothes. Hungry, but too tired to cook, we celebrated reaching loon country with a jar of pickled herring, crackers topped with cheddar cheese, and one of the beers. We decided to leave the bunk beds and mattresses to their present occupants, which we took from the obvious signs to be packrats and mice. We spread our sleeping bags out on the wooden floor, turned off the lantern, and went to sleep.

I awoke an hour later as a mouse ran across my hand, and I listened for a while to the nocturnal sounds of little animals scurrying around the old fishing shack. Finally I fell asleep again, only to be reawakened by a great gnawing sound from outside the door. I slowly opened the screen door and shone the flashlight onto the wooden steps. A large brown, summer-coated snowshoe hare with huge white feet was nibbling on the steps. It took one look

*In thick forest surrounding a wilderness lake, a red squirrel peers cautiously from its tree home. Like other animals of the north that do not migrate or hibernate, the squirrel busily stores food for the approaching winter.*

*A common loon chick follows its parent through the reflections of their wilderness surroundings. Chicks will often ride on the adult's back since their own downy feathers get easily soaked.*

## *notes from the field* (continued)

at me and hopped gently away. By now Kathy was awake and wondering what was going on. I told her, leaving out the part about the mouse running over my hand, and she immediately dragged her sleeping bag out the door to a grassy area in front of the cabin. Mosquitoes had invaded the woods as the evening breeze had died down, so at 4 a.m., shortly before daybreak, we pitched our tent in front of the cabin. As I drifted off to sleep, I wondered if there really were any loons on this lake. Thirty minutes later, at the first sign of daylight, I heard my answer— the unmistakable yodeling call of a pair of loons directly in front of our camp. It was as if they had come to greet us.

I hoped that the difficult part of this expedition was over and that I could get to work photographing loons. Eventually, Kathy and I did observe and photograph four different loon families!

We enjoyed our five days out on the lake, exploring its coves and the little streams that flowed into it. Every morning at sunrise, we would see amber-colored dots glowing on the far eastern shoreline. We discovered these to be white-tailed deer feeding on the succulent grasses in the shallows along the shore. We would see them only for the first half-hour of daylight, and then they would disappear. One day we rounded a point and saw one of the deer a hundred yards from shore. The sleek young buck with velvet antlers watched us as though he'd never seen a boat or humans before, then raised his tail and leaped gracefully through the water and back to cover. We each shot a series of pictures which, as often happens, turned out to be at least as special as those we had come for. I'll never forget the image of the largest bull moose I have ever seen, although I didn't get a picture of him. He was in a wooded cove at twilight, standing shoulder deep and raising his massive velvet-covered antlers out of the water as he fed on submerged plants. The loons, the deer, the moose, even the carpet of wild daisies around the shack, are not only on film, but etched in our memories. By the end of our stay on this wild northern lake, I had learned where the rocky shoals were, and I had no more thought of trading jobs with anyone.

*FOLLOWING PAGES*

*Western sandpipers follow the Pacific coastline of Washington as they migrate north in the spring. These sandpipers will nest only along the coast of western and northern Alaska, but in winter will spread out from California to South America.*

With its powerful feet and
talons outstretched to pluck
a salmon from the water, a
bald eagle skims the calm
surface of a spawning
stream.

Sunlight accents the pure
white feathers and yellow
beak of a mature bald eagle
as it rests in a spruce tree.
From its high perch, the
eagle watches for fish or
other prey below.

*A brant feather lost in the late summer molt is all that remains of the migrating birds when the first autumn storm comes to the Alaskan coast.*

*Migrating whimbrels gather on the rocks of a Pacific bay. The whimbrel is a medium-sized curlew that nests in the northern tundra and winters as far south as Chile.*

*An arctic tern rests briefly before taking to the air again. In the course of nesting in the arctic and wintering in the seas of Antarctica, the arctic tern may fly up to 22,000 miles a year.*

*A familiar sound along Alaskan coasts is the call of the song sparrow coming from low, dense vegetation. The song sparrow prefers to live near water, and its various subspecies are found across the entire continent.*

# HIGHLANDS
## *images of mountain and forest*

. . . . . . . . . . . . . . . . . . . . . . . . . . . . . . . . . .

*The deep red of mountain maple is one of the brightest autumn colors in the western mountains. Aspen trees, with their soft white bark, are just beginning to turn deep yellow.*

*With its feathers puffed up in minus-twenty-degree weather, a Bohemian waxwing displays the red, waxy tips of its wing feathers that give waxwings their name.*

Where the granite spine of North America is exposed and weathered lies a world of dense pine forests, lakes, rivers, and sculptured peaks. The high country is a rich nesting and birthing ground in summer and a quiet land of snow and bare subsistence in winter. It is the retreat of plains animals displaced by man, the realm of the few remaining great predators and concentrated herds of prey. Here, ecological variety offers niches to countless shapes and sizes of life, from water lilies in glacier scoured ponds to mountain sheep on windy, high crags. In the brief flush of life that is the highland summer, colorful and delicate birds such as the mountain bluebird and western tanager arrive to nest and raise young. Seasons change quickly, and life adapts to the transformation of the landscape. When winter mantles the land, animals must move, adapt, or hibernate. Many do leave for warmer climates or lower elevations and find new winter food, others change their coloring for seasonal camouflage. Herds of grazing animals find open, windswept hillsides where the vegetation is cleared of snow. The

. . . . . . . . . . . . . . . . . . . . . . . . . . . . . . . . . .

Water lilies cover a shallow
pond in northern Montana.
As glaciers of the Ice Age
retreated, they left buried in
the soil many chunks of ice
that eventually melted to
form ponds or potholes.

One of the most colorful
birds of the Rocky Mountain
pine and spruce forests, the
western tanager was first
described by Lewis and
Clark on their exploration
of the West.

*An unsuspecting salmon is
pulled from its spawning
bed by a bald eagle. Thousands of fish gathering in
shallow headwaters to lay
their eggs attract predators
like the bald eagle.*

*November snow dusts
a spruce tree and the
numerous bald eagles
perched on its limbs. When
the spawning salmon are
gone, the eagles will
continue their migration to
their wintering areas.*

*PRECEDING PAGES
A flock of Bohemian and
cedar waxwings descends
on a berry-laden mountain
ash tree. The nutritious
berries are a favorite of
waxwings, which nest late to
harvest the ripe berries for
their fledging young.*

# BALD EAGLE
## notes from the field

Kokanee are a landlocked race of sockeye salmon that inhabit Flathead Lake in western Montana. For many years great numbers of these kokanee would migrate during their fall spawning season up into the streams that empty into Flathead Lake. Here they would find the shallow water where they had hatched and lay their own eggs. Although the fish population is currently low from environmental disturbance or natural cyclic conditions, at one time their numbers were great. One of the streams where the salmon spawned is McDonald Creek in Glacier National Park, a slow-moving, meandering stream that drains Lake McDonald in the west end of the park.

McDonald Creek winds back and forth across the flat floor of the steep-sided valley. The side hills are covered with dense stands of tamarack and spruce, and the valley floor is covered with willows and scattered, tall spruce trees.

From late October to late November, McDonald Creek was full of salmon, and the annual event had attracted many wild animals that came to catch and feed on the fish. The most numerous and conspicuous to congregate here was the bald eagle, with 400 to 600 of the raptors in the narrow valley during peak years. They would spend the day perched in trees along the river, swooping down to catch salmon and carrying them to a snag to feed. On an average day each eagle would catch and eat half a dozen fish. At sundown the eagles would fly across Lake McDonald to roost in a grove of cottonwoods. When the spawning ended the eagles would continue on their migration.

I spent each day from daylight to dusk on a bridge that crossed the creek, watching and photographing the eagles. I began to focus my attention on their favorite perches and fishing spots, and I learned their daily cycles of feeding and resting. If the temperature was twenty to thirty degrees below zero, the eagles would stay perched all day. On those days I would watch the banks of the creek to find other animals attracted to the bounty. Coyotes would sneak out to grab salmon splashing near shore, and grizzlies would leave their tracks in the snow where they came at night to eat fish. Even white-tailed deer waded out to eat an occasional salmon.

71

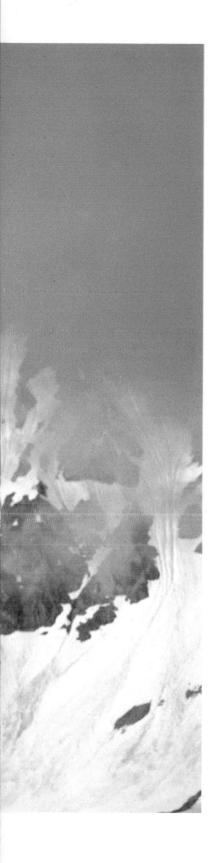

*The slopes of a glacier-scarred mountain form a cold backdrop for a bald eagle soaring in spring winds. From this height, the eagle can spot fish or other eagles feeding many miles away in the narrow valley.*

*A pair of bald eagles arrives at their nesting territory in early spring to begin court-ship. They return each year to the same nest, adding sticks until it may be as much as eight feet in width.*

*Yellowstone's first winter*
*storm mantles a bull elk*
*and his harem in the*
*meadow where they nap.*
*As the mating season ends*
*and snows deepen, the elk*
*will move to lower valleys*
*and open hillsides.*

*Sunrise reveals a cow elk*
*seeking out fresh green*
*shoots on the banks of the*
*Yellowstone River.*

# ELK AND COYOTE
## *notes from the field*

At the end of October, Yellowstone Park was about to close for the winter. It had snowed sixteen inches in three days and the entire park had suddenly become quiet, as if the animal life were waiting to see if this was the arrival of deepest winter.

I found a small band of elk in a very serene setting. It was the end of the mating season, and a large bull had his harem of cows and calves bedded down in a sheltered meadow. The weather was extremely variable—snowing hard one minute, sunny the next. When I found the herd of elk, they were coated with a blanket of fresh snow where they lay in the meadow, and the sun was breaking through the storm with a clean, soft light. I had taken a few photographs of the elk bedded down when the bull got up to bugle an answer to another bull off in the timber a half-mile away. Their challenges echoed through the meadow, then the snowfall returned, and the meadow became quiet again.

That afternoon I saw a coyote cross the road ahead of me as I was leaving the park. She had beautiful, thick fur and looked ready for winter. As she started to hunt for mice I followed along on foot. She obviously knew I was no threat to her, and would ignore me as long as I kept my distance. I stayed with her for several hours, catching her in different poses as she hunted along the edges of the lodgepole pine forest and through steamy thermal areas. By the time it started getting dark, I had shot six rolls of film. When I turned to go back to the car I realized that I had been so intent on the coyote that I wasn't sure which direction to go. I had to follow our tracks back to the road and in doing that I came to appreciate how many miles a coyote covers in its zigzag course to find food.

*Among the most adaptable and persistent mountain predators are the coyotes. The valleys often echo at night with their howling and yelping chorus.*

*Originally a plains animal, the elk has retreated to high mountain meadows and forests. As the first snow arrives, this bull elk bugles a challenge to rivals for control of his harem of cows.*

*FOLLOWING PAGES*
*Ice on a Yukon lake slowly recedes with the arrival of spring. The colors of the sunset last for hours as the season of continual daylight approaches.*

*A greater sandhill crane
leads its chick toward the
grass where it will find its
first meal of insects.*

*A three-day-old sandhill
crane colt stands in a bed
of lupine. Within two
months, the young crane
will have grown to be nearly
four feet tall.*

*With its incredibly sharp
eyesight and hearing, the
great gray owl locates mice
in the grass below its perch.
These owls hunt in the
morning and evening and
in more northern forests
during the day.*

*The forest-dwelling great
gray owl, the largest of
North American owls,
locates its prey with its
facial disc of feathers acting
as a parabolic reflector that
gathers and pinpoints
sound.*

# GREAT GRAY OWL
## notes from the field

· · · · · · · · · · · · · · · · · · · · · · · ·

I hear stories from people who come into my photography gallery about wildlife they have seen. Different visitors were relaying reports to me of a great gray owl observed catching mice in a particular meadow near the Snake River. By the fourth report, I realized there must be a nesting pair of owls that hunted there regularly.

I went out for six evenings and sat on a hillside above the meadow and watched until dusk. The meadow was in a clearing at the edge of the river bottom where a thick blue spruce forest grew, and each day just at dusk one of the owls would fly out of the forest to land in a few scattered aspen trees to hunt for mice and voles. Great gray owls are typically not shy, and by the third day they were accustomed to seeing me. I would move slowly and never approach them directly, and they began to ignore me. It was a very peaceful and silent arrangement in the meadow, with the lengthening shadows and the silent flight of the owls in the calm air.

· · · · · · · · · · · · · · · · · · · · · · · ·

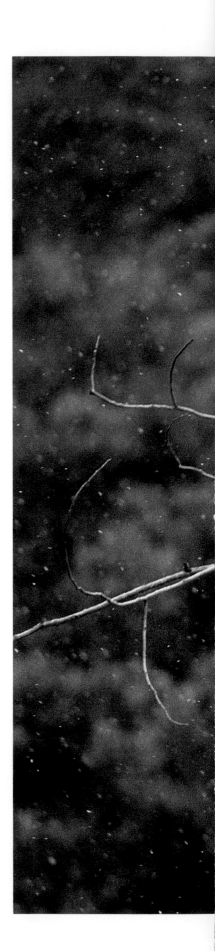

*With his antlers gathering
snow, a bull moose naps in
the river-bottom land where
he winters. His long legs
enable him to travel through
deep snow to feed on the
shoots and buds of willows.*

*One resident of the boreal
forest who remains through-
out the year is the great gray
owl, but in especially hard,
snowy winters, the owls will
migrate south to the limits
of their forests.*

*FOLLOWING PAGES
The first heavy snowfall of
winter blankets a bull
moose in his willow-thicket
home.*

Perched in an alder over-
looking a beaver pond, a
belted kingfisher watches
until the moment when it
will dive underwater to
grab a fish in its powerful
bill.

Cloud patterns of an
August sunrise are
reflected in a wide bend of
the Yellowstone River.

*Aspen trees grow on the lower slopes of the Rockies, where their first tinge of autumn color contrasts with surrounding evergreens. They are called "quaking aspens" because their leaves rustle in the slightest breeze.*

*Fireweed often appears in spectacular blooms that cover meadows and burned or disturbed areas. The tall plants are eaten by deer, elk, and grizzly bears.*

# GRASSLAND
## *images of prairie and stream*

A dry wind bends the tall grass in waves as it follows the rounded contours of the land, rolling and curling mile after mile. It whistles in the low shrubs, raises dust from exposed hillsides, and sways the tops of trees that grow protected in ravines and along meandering streams. To the north a range of hills breaks the flat plain. In the bottom of a broad valley is a stream that drained away centuries of melting glacier. Tall trees grow along its banks, out of the path of spring floods that carry soil worn from the distant mountains. Animal life is of two kinds: creatures that hide or burrow in the thick mat of grass and roots, and those that move swiftly above it. Low in the southern sky, a flock of sandhill cranes beats slowly into the wind of the last spring snowstorm. The north wind that has swept unimpeded across miles of unbroken land buffets the cranes as they bank sharply and set their wings to descend into the river valley. They glide over cottonwood trees and down into the wide river channel where they pass over ducks and geese to land on a flat sandbar. Over the cranes flies a small flock of pintail ducks in a

*When cyclical populations of their prey reach low levels, snowy owls often appear in the farm country of Alberta, Canada, in search of food. A granary built in the 1930s serves as an observation perch.*

*The powerful snowy owl watches from a fencepost for prey. In the absence of its preferred diet of lemmings, the displaced arctic bird will hunt rabbits and weasels and will even attack animals caught in traps.*

# SNOWY OWL
## *notes from the field*

. . . . . . . . . . . . . . . . . . . . . . . .

Snowy owls are normally found in the arctic tundra, nesting on the treeless ground in moss and lichens. But in severe winters they are driven far south in their search for food and often end up in southern Canada and the northern United States. I was in the wheat-farm country of southeastern Alberta in January, trying to photograph the owls that had migrated there. I saw up to six a day but could not get close enough for the image I wanted. I kept seeing the big white owls sitting on fenceposts or straw bales, but in the flat wheatfields I knew I couldn't get near enough to the skittish birds before they would fly off. Even with the use of a long telephoto lens the image of the owl would be too small unless combined with another interesting element. I visualized how great it would be to see an owl on top of one of the decrepit grain storage sheds, built in the 1930s, that dotted the landscape.

I had just about given up for the day and was driving back toward town when I saw the white shape of an owl sitting on the peak of an old granary a mile from the road. There were only about twenty minutes of light left and the temperature was minus 35 degrees, so I grabbed my camera and started walking quickly out toward the granary. I followed a zigzag course, never going directly toward the owl, and I reached an adjacent granary without scaring the bird. I hid in the granary for several minutes and warmed my camera under my coat, and then I peered out. I could tell from the whitewash of droppings on the granary that the bird perched there often, and I knew it would be reluctant to fly off into the intense cold. I stepped out into the open, and the owl looked directly at me. I assumed it was used to the farmer who visited the granaries, so I pretended to ignore the owl and moved slowly out into the field for a better angle. The owl turned its gaze away from me, and I had time to shoot ten exposures before the light faded.

. . . . . . . . . . . . . . . . . . . . . . . .

*Lacking powerf*
*hold its prey, th*
*shrike, a preda*
*bird, impales its*
*securely on a th*
*barbed wire.*

*A mixture of fo*
*yarrow bends i*
*wind. Foxtail b*
*cause blindness*
*grazing anima*
*yarrow was use*
*Americans as a*

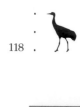

*Migrating tundra swans prepare for a landing in a shallow prairie pond. Previously named whistling swans, they are marked with a yellow teardrop shape on the base of their black bills.*

*Running along the surface of the water, the heavy trumpeter swan uses the distance to work up a full wingbeat to lift itself into the air.*

*PRECEDING PAGES Tundra swans nest on dry tundra near water in Alaska and winter along both coasts of the United States. Their long migrations carry them across the continent twice a year.*

*Some of the last herds of bison have found refuge in the wooded canyons and plateaus of the prairies, where deep snow forces them to move in search of new grazing. Bison use their massive heads to sweep the ground clear of snow.*

*Canada geese mate for life, and the pairs remain together even as winter covers their northern nesting grounds and they migrate south.*

*The red-bellied woodpecker
lives in thick forest along
river bottoms, where it flies
from tree to tree to hammer
into the wood after insect
larvae.*

*Cardinals live and continue
to sing in their brushy home
year-round, even in the
coldest weather. The males
become fiercely territorial
in the spring.*

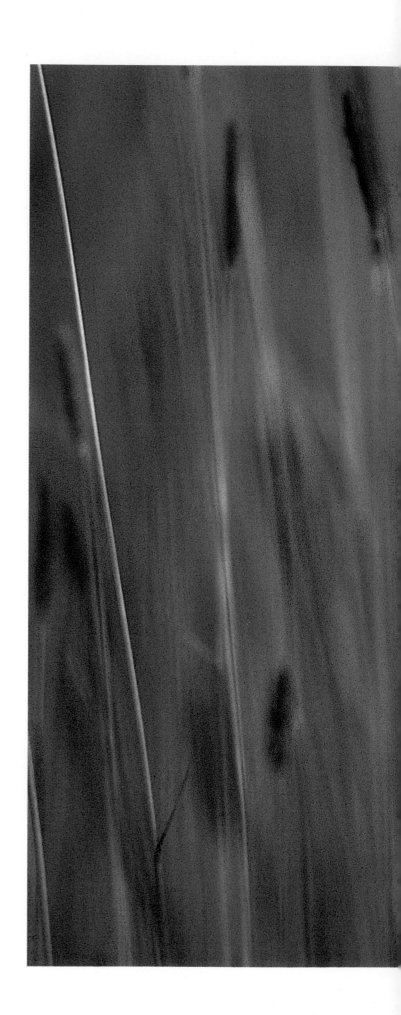

*Stepping through shallow
water in a prairie marsh,
an American avocet feeds
by sweeping its slender,
upcurved bill from side to
side as it wades.*

*A resident of fields and
open country, the American
goldfinch, sometimes called
the thistle bird, feeds on
the seeds of grasses, wild-
flowers, and thistles.*

*The goldfinch nests late in the season after most other birds have fledged in order to take advantage of the seeds of thistles and other late summer plants.*

*Huge flocks of up to 200,000 snow geese winter in the river valleys of the southern prairies. The most abundant of wild geese, they nest in large colonies in the arctic tundra.*

*Found in wooded gullies
and forested bottomland
scattered across the prairies,
the great horned owl, a
large and powerful preda-
tor, hoots a deep call that
carries over considerable
distances in the night.*

*Winter on the prairies finds
a small band of pronghorns
looking for protection from
the wind. As the fastest
North American animal,
and with their sharp vision,
pronghorns are well
adapted to open country.*

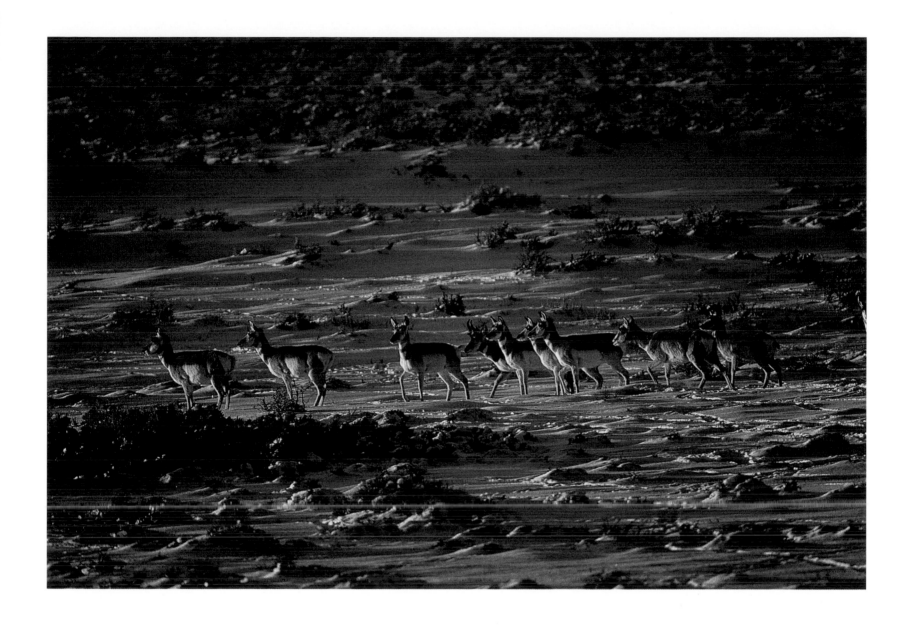

*FOLLOWING PAGES*
*Each year, thousands of*
*sandhill cranes gather in*
*staging areas for their long*
*spring migration to Alaska*
*and Siberia.*

*Canada geese return to
their nest island in May to
find their pond still frozen
and a fresh dusting of snow
on the ground. They will
defend the island, and the
female will build her nest of
grass and down.*

*The Platte River in
Nebraska has been used by
migrating sandhill cranes
for millions of years. Each
evening, thousands of
cranes return to roost after
feeding in surrounding
fields and meadows.*

# PRAIRIE WATERFOWL
*notes from the field*

My earliest memories are those of the prairies. I remember sitting on the steps of our house in Grand Island, Nebraska, watching my dad come home from hunting with a half-dozen mallards draped around his neck. He would lift the string of heavy drakes over his head and place them at my feet. I was fascinated by their feathers, iridescent green heads, and hard yellowish bills.

My initiation to the prairie world of the Platte River came when I was four. I remember climbing into the brown tin boat filled with the wooden duck and goose decoys Dad had made. On top of the decoys he laid his 12-gauge shotgun and a small army knapsack that contained his duck and goose calls, extra shotgun shells, thermos bottle of coffee, and our lunch of peanut butter sandwiches.

We would leave the south bank of the Platte River in the dark an hour or more before sunrise. So he wouldn't scare any roosting birds, Dad wouldn't use his flashlight once we had started towards the blind, which was a half-mile away through flooded willows and across the open river. He didn't need the light; he had come here every day of the season. At that hour the air was alive with the sounds of ducks and geese moving up and down the river. I could hear the rush of wings and their chattering feed calls overhead and would look up to see only stars in the darkness above. It was an exciting time for me.

Dad's blind consisted of four oaken pickle barrels sunk in the ground on a little willow-covered island in the middle of the channel. Dad had hunted on this island or one nearby since 1932, when he was sixteen. Almost forty years later, my first photographs would be taken from this same blind.

Every day and every year on the river was a new learning experience. The weather more than anything influenced the behavior of the birds and our hunting techniques. Warm, sunny days with south breezes were best for geese, while cold, overcast days with blustery north winds brought the mallards down. When heavy snow blanketed the grain fields of the Dakotas to the north, both ducks and geese would funnel into the Platte. I have vivid memories of those days when we would see flight after flight of migrating waterfowl.

By the end of October most of the pintails, widgeon,

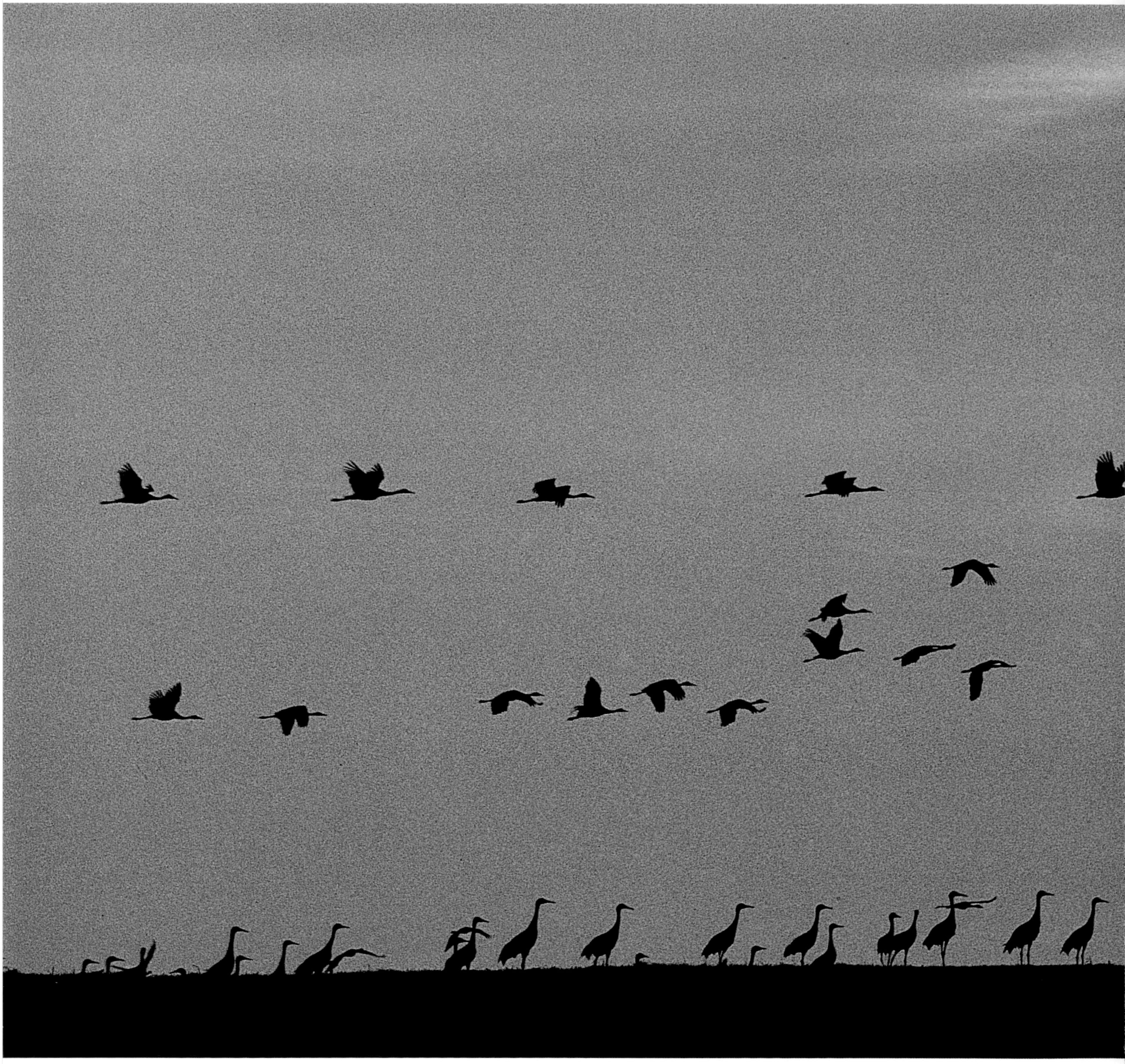

*Whooping cranes migrate in small groups to Wood Buffalo Park in Canada's Northwest Territories, where their only nesting ground remains.*

*A broad-winged hawk that soars over open country, the Swainson's hawk eats chiefly mice and large insects. These hawks gather in tremendous flocks during their annual fall migration to South America.*

*Reflections of summer
foliage surround the striking
male wood duck on a creek
near its nest. Wood ducks
nest in tree hollows, often
high off the ground, and
adapt easily to boxes placed
in farm ponds.*

*An iridescent green head
marks the drake mallard,
one of the best-known
ducks.*

# TUNDRA
## *images of the north*

. . . . . . . . . . . . . . . . . . . . . . . . . . . .

The spring sun first gleams over the low horizon, and winter begins to lift slowly from the barren regions of the north. Within weeks the rolling tundra and the low ridges begin to warm as the sun arcs higher and longer each day. The mountains that erupt from the smooth landscape will hold their cold snow and ice all year, but on gentle hillsides and rocky outcroppings the increasing heat of the sun melts snow, uncovering lichens and mosses, and life stirs. In a small valley the trickle of water is audible through the last ice and snow covering a stream. Willows begin to emerge from the snow drifts and a gaunt young moose finds new strength in their exposed shoots. Having survived his first winter alone, he slowly works his way several miles downstream toward the broad expanse of a river bottom filled with willow and sedge. The clear spring air is cold, and the first sounds of life carry across the open country. In a wide river basin a small herd of caribou moves up onto the surrounding hillsides. Their long winter diet of lichens and moss has left them thin, and they search

. . . . . . . . . . . . . . . . . . . . . . . . . . . .

*Taiga forest and tundra in fall colors surround a lake where a pair of tundra swans feed. The birds nest away from water in the dense mat of moss and grass that covers the arctic ground.*

*On their way to find fresh grazing, three Dall sheep cross the rock debris of a talus slope in the rugged Alaska range. When winter arrives, the sheep move to lower, windblown hillsides where they can find exposed vegetation.*

On the ornately symmetrical
antlers of the caribou, a
velvet covering supplies
blood for antler growth.
This dries when the antlers
mature and is rubbed off
by the time of the fall
mating season.

Leaving its winter range, a
bull caribou seeks out fresh
green vegetation to supply
the nutrients needed for
antler growth.

*As the changing colors of
tundra vegetation testify,
the arctic summer is coming
to an end for this tiny wood
frog.*

*Winter temperatures and scarcity of food take their toll on the herds of caribou. The winter-killed animals are scavenged by foxes, ravens, and grizzlies in the spring.*

# ANCIENT PLAINS
## *images of Africa*

*Sunrise near Buffalo Springs, Kenya, accentuates the shape of an acacia tree. Nocturnal predators find their day beds as the sky brightens and the plains come to life.*

*A pair of white-throated bee eaters watches for bees and wasps to fly near. The birds fly off their perch to pluck their prey from the air, then return to their perch and repeatedly knock the bee against a limb until it discharges all its venom.*

An African landscape slowly takes shape in the dim light of early morning. The first hint of sunrise on the distant horizon reveals an outline of worn and rounded hills and, beyond that, the massive, ancient volcanic mountains. As the sky grows light, details of the Serengeti plain begin to show. The crowns of thorny acacia trees are silhouetted against the sunrise, and egrets and cranes roosting in the trees stretch their wings and look for signs of movement out on the grassy plains. The barking of jackals from a dry riverbed mixes with the chorus of bird life awakening in the forest. Within minutes every detail of the immense landscape is unveiled in the clear morning air. The rich, green grass that stretches smoothly to the mountainous horizon is broken by scattered stands of trees and herd after herd of grazing animals. The sky is as vast as the land; to the east it begins to fill with billowy cumulus clouds. Sky, grassland, and animals seem to flow in parallel planes from horizon to horizon as the first morning breeze stirs. The clouds drift, the life-giving grass sways, and gazelle and wildebeest

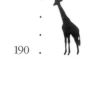

*Although the leopard hunts mostly in the forest at night, the spotted pattern of its coat makes it nearly invisible to other animals when it stalks in the grass during the day.*

*A leopard watches the movements of a herd of gazelles. If successful in a kill, it will drag its prey into the tree where scavengers cannot reach it.*

*In the bush and acacia tree
country, a pair of secretary
birds stands on the thorny
perch where they will build
their nest. A terrestrial bird
of prey that eats snakes and
rodents, the secretary bird
is the only species in its
distinct family.*

*A small herd of beautiful
impalas feeds and finds
relief from the sun in the
shade of an acacia.
Cheetahs and leopards are
their chief predators.*

*Despite being abundant,*
*Burchell's zebras remain*
*one of the most striking*
*sights of the African plains.*
*Small groups and families*
*join together to form large*
*herds for protection against*
*predators.*

*PRECEDING PAGES*
*Grevy's zebras near Buffalo*
*Springs, Kenya, are identi-*
*fied by their many narrow*
*stripes and large, rounded*
*ears. At a distance, the*
*Grevy's zebra appears*
*brownish and blends into*
*the vegetation.*

*An old termite mound is home and vantage point for a family of cheetahs. Although the cheetah, the fastest land animal, is capable of seventy-five miles an hour, it tires quickly, and so it stealthily moves within striking distance of its prey.*

*As an approaching storm darkens the sky, lions roam in Masai Mara, Kenya. Lions are the most diurnal of the large cats and often move about to set up daytime ambushes for prey.*

*Years of prairie wind and
weather have taken their
toll on a neglected barn,
where a pair of sparrows
seeks refuge on a cold
January day.*

# PHOTOGRAPHY NOTES

. . . . . . . . . . . . . . . . . . . . . . . . . . . . . . . . . . . .

Many times I am asked, "What kind of equipment and film do you use?" Nearly all of my photographs are made with a 35mm Nikon camera. I bought my first camera twenty years ago and the Nikon system is the one I became most familiar with; however, I do not believe it matters a great deal which camera system one uses. Great pictures are made everyday with many different cameras and lenses. What does matter is being able to respond immediately and effectively with the equipment one has at any given picture opportunity. The three most important lenses to me are the 24mm, 85mm and the 300mm. When I go into the field, I carry these lenses along with a 1.4x tele converter, and two camera bodies with motor drives. In the car, or on a major trip, I may also include an 80-200mm, a 400mm, and a 600mm lens. I would take along plenty of Kodachrome 64 for sunny days, enough Fujichrome 100 for overcast days, and a few rolls of Kodachrome 200 for days or places of little light.

Knowing the subject you intend to photograph is very important, but the subject may not always be the most important element in a picture. To me, the quality of light surrounding the subject is generally more important than the subject itself. Light gives detail, texture and mood to a scene. The best light is often thought to be that early morning or late evening "magic hour" light, but it may also be midday light filtered through fog, clouds, or the leaves of a forest.

Images with the simplest design or pattern are usually the pictures that are most personally satisfying to me. One of my favorite images—of a barn and sparrows—best sums up how the above elements come together with the actual photographic process. On a cold January 1st in 1975 while hunting pheasants in southeast Nebraska, I saw the old barn standing near the top of a hill. The light was low, but it added to the loneliness and nostalgia of the scene. I had only one camera, my first Nikon FTN, and a 55mm macro lens which is generally used for close-up photography. As I stepped into the plowed field, I glimpsed the two sparrows racing to the open door of the barn. In less than three seconds, I set the shutter speed at one five-hundredth of a second to "freeze" their flight, I estimated the corresponding f/stop of the lens, composed, focused, and pressed the shutter release.

As I conclude these final notes, I am distracted by the dozen rosy-colored Cassin's finches at the feeder, and by thoughts of how fortunate I have been to see so much. Thoughts of whales, and the animals of Africa, species of the rain forests and the old growth forests, and the birds and mammals of the Platte River and Prince William Sound. Wild, precious, delicate places. The sun is beginning to burn through the fog and a hole in the clouds reveals the fresh snow on the peaks of the Tetons. I think ahead to tomorrow and the images it will bring.

. . . . . . . . . . . . . . . . . . . . . . . . . . . . . . . . . . . .